I0101559

The Apprentice and the Project Manager

Lessons for Developing an Agile Mindset

By Kamal Manglani

Happy About

20660 Stevens Creek Blvd., Suite 210
Cupertino, CA 95014

Copyright © 2014 by Kamal Manglani

All rights reserved. No part of this book shall be reproduced, stored in a retrieval system, or transmitted by any means electronic, mechanical, photocopying, recording, or otherwise without written permission from the publisher.

Published by Happy About®, a THiNKaha® imprint
20660 Stevens Creek Blvd., Suite 210,
Cupertino, CA 95014
http://happyabout.com

First Printing: March 2014
Paperback ISBN: 978-1-60005-252-1 (1-60005-252-5)
eBook ISBN: 978-1-60005-253-8 (1-60005-253-3)
Place of Publication: Silicon Valley, California, USA
Paperback Library of Congress Number: 2014900459

Trademarks

All terms mentioned in this book that are known to be trademarks or service marks have been appropriately capitalized. Neither THiNKaha®, (the parent company of Happy About®) nor any of its imprints, can attest to the accuracy of this information. Use of a term in this book should not be regarded as affecting the validity of any trademark or service mark.

Warning and Disclaimer

This work is not reflective of experiences with any company or place. It is purely a fictional narrative and the work is not related to any person, living or dead.

Every effort has been made to make this book as complete and as accurate as possible. The information provided is on an "as is" basis. The author(s), publisher, and their agents assume no responsibility for errors or omissions. Nor do they assume liability or responsibility to any person or entity with respect to any loss or damages arising from the use of information contained herein.

Advance Praises

"The Apprentice and the Project Manager *by Kamal Manglani is an entertaining read with a serious message. The author tells the story through the eyes of the apprentice at an auto workshop who then applies the lessons learned to his new job as an IT project manager at a candy manufacturer. The narrative provides a strong introduction to developing an agile mindset and how today's companies can unblock their overstretched IT department to start realizing value fast. Manglani's style is reminiscent of the late, great Eli Goldratt and shares Goldratt's ability to make the complex seem simple.*"
Greg Cohen, Author of *"Agile Excellence for Product Managers"*

"It's just like what Kamal mentioned at the beginning: 'Small changes that make big mindset shift happen.' This book will let people understand how important it is to be positive, to keep the passion of learning, and [to realize] what makes you stop before you achieve your fullest potential. The best thing of this book is it is made up of different stories, and I can find almost all the answers from reading the stories. And furthermore, it will lead you to re-examine and deeply question yourself, and that is the start for change."
Congcong Li, Branch Manager and Senior Business Analyst in LTS

"The Apprentice and the Project Manager *takes complex business issues to core principles that can be easily understood, and provides examples that marketing and development teams can use. The book is organized as a number of lessons that are easily understood in the physical world, but are quickly forgotten in the software world. Kamal Manglani's book reminds the reader of the fundamental principles and business values that are often forgotten when enterprise-level complexity is added.* The Apprentice and the Project Manager *is a good read, whether you are on your first agile journey, or an experienced agilest looking for a fun reminder."*

Terry Quan, Partner, EAmmune

"The application of Agile and Lean Principles can sometimes be misunderstood and confused along the way to understanding the value of the application of these principles. Kamal Manglani has created a clever method of illustrating both industry and consumer situations that can be improved by the application of Agile and Lean principles. In this book, the perspective of both the customer and the organization are reflected within the examples. What is clear in the book is the benefit of the value gained by both the customer and the organization after the application of Agile and Lean principles. Practical situations where the understanding of measurement and Work In Progress help to qualify a problem prior to the application of Agile and Lean are identified in this book. There is even a chapter that

discusses *Value stream mapping in financial terms. Overall, this book is a great way to be introduced to the practical understanding and the need/benefit of the application of Agile and Lean principles.*"
Steve Colasinski,Enterprise Agile Coach for Fortune 100 companies

"*Through the use of story, Manglani cuts through the textbook learning and demonstrates applied principals that any reader can relate to. The juxtaposition of the auto shop against the corporate environment effectively demonstrates that the insights Manglani shares are not restricted solely to any one industry. A recommended read for any professional wishing to bring value to their lives and workplace environments through the adoption of an agile mindset.*"
Michael Sutherland, Programs Manager

"*For me, excelling in business is mostly about insights. Insight today rarely comes from the academic heavy books. However, today I personally get most of my insights in conversations with senior business executives. People who know what they are doing and love what they do. This book in particular belongs to that crowd of sources who want to influence or want to sharpen their influencing skills through story telling applicable to real life. This book is a great metric that inspires my behavior to form new habits and be inspired to increase value!*"
Erik Olsson, Director of Business Development

"There are pearls of wisdom in this book that is a wonderful quick read. Most importantly, I was able to identify my work in technology consulting with it very closely, and the book explains very simple, but powerful lessons that I was able to implement right away at my workplace to solve real world challenges."
Mahesh Gollamudi, Business Process Consultant

"Great lessons on identifying value by reducing waste. This book is a quick read. Highly actionable lessons that go beyond technology and useful for the modern professional regardless of industry."
Kaizad Cassad, Solicitor Advocate and Accredited Mediator (England & Wales and India)

"This is a fantastic book for people at all levels in a company who are looking for very useful insights to create more value for projects and enhance company equity. By reading this book, I have found many practical concepts that are directly applicable in my daily work and life. You will miss a lot if you don't read it. I cannot wait for part 2."
Pai-Li Lin, Product Manager

"This book brings Agile and Lean out of the software and manufacturing world and makes it applicable to every business. This book and the actions to tweet allow the user to be more engaged with the story while teaching a few more esoteric ideas in Agile. I expect and look forward to seeing more."

Stuart Mc Calla, Agile Coach and Team Liberator

"If you have ever been on a failed business or technology project, this is a must-read book! This work will help you relate to some very powerful, yet simple-to-understand lessons on Lean. The short story format keeps the pace and helps you learn quickly. Kudos to Manglani for being able to draw examples from two different lines of business and provide frameworks to looking at common leadership issues."

Navjot Singh, Director-Business Development Verveba Telecom

"I love the parable writing style. Reading a story that you're interested in with simple lessons learned told as part of the story. Kamal hits the nail on the head with this book. Simple, interesting story, powerful lessons learned that apply not only to agile project management, but to the way business needs to run today."

Mitchell Levy, Thought Leader Architect & CEO, THiNKaha

Dedication

This work is dedicated to technology professionals who have a desire to shift the mindset in their companies and their lives.

The book also attempts to encourage everyone to observe as an apprentice, or "one who is very open to learning." This is an important skill we must possess when about to start a career. Arming oneself with keen powers of observation and listening will enable greater outcomes. This work reminds us that learning options, such as apprenticeships and internships, exist. They are perhaps the optimal means to learning and building a successful career plan, which, in this case, is a Leader with a Lean, or Agile, Mindset.

Goal

This book is purely a fictional narrative with simple, but powerful stories that help one understand the small changes that can make a big mindset shift happen. The author's personal goal is to enable people to realize that all change starts with a simple shift in mindset.

Contents

Introduction

The chapters that follow are about the experiences of an apprentice in an auto workshop, who learns the various types of optimizations, and expands them to be applied in his corporate job. They are similar to what is defined as Lean IT, though currently called an Agile mindset, and essentially are short, iterative cycles of work in order to change Behavior to focus on outcomes (not just outputs), and to continue on the path, until there is significant value compared to the costs of the outcome.

It is easy to spot physical excess in our environment. We have optimized ways to manage these wastes with the use of full scale systems. Imagine if the litter in your city was not removed for a month. This would pose a serious problem. There is huge amount of waste in software development, and until we develop an intuitive mindset to gather awareness, we will never be able to manage it all. This will eventually cause companies to slowly turn into non-high-performing ones.

The apprentice is hired to help out at an auto shop that is severely constrained in terms of resources. However, once a mindset shift is seeded, the auto shop uses the same constraints as strategic levers to develop with unprecedented growth. These are simple practices that can be adapted overnight, as long as the right seeds have been planted in our organizations for mindset shift.

Short cycles are important to measure, observe, and reflect the behaviors causing the measures to go positive or negative. If we have long periods of work cycles without sufficient reflections, it becomes even more difficult to measure, and thus, the behavior shift never happens or is very difficult.

Behavior shift is necessary to make a habit of winning. Companies will only develop such a habit if they learn quickly from failures.

At the beginning of each chapter is a simple Tweet. Please tweet the sentence if you want to share the message with more minds. At the end of each chapter is a brief lesson covering the material learned.

Each chapter is split in two time periods. One is the teenage years where the main central character is an apprentice in an auto shop. Then follows the present years, where he transitions to a Project Manager in the IT department of a candy company, and gradually makes his way up to senior executive levels.

Outline of each chapter

Tweet message #...

Time period Teenage... (Interchangeable)

....
....
....

Time period Current years...(Interchangeable)

Lesson Learned...

Characters in the Book:

John – Time-pressed customer that drives a high end car

Jack – Our star technician

Me – The Apprentice – Our central character in an auto workshop (in the past)

Me – The Project Manager – Our central character in the present, working at a candy manufacturing company.

Mike – Owner of the auto workshop

Stan – The savior of the auto workshop and a brother of Mike

Steve – Materials manager at the auto workshop

Lynda – Portfolio Manager at the candy company

1 The Auto Apprentice & the Project Manager

Tweet: *Failure is imminent, but it's important to learn from mistakes in order to succeed sooner. @ApprenticePM*

During my teenage years, I had the opportunity to be both an apprentice and manager at a local auto workshop. The workshop was in a neighborhood among many others providing the exact same services on cars or other automobiles. Every day, the technicians would show up in the morning at eight and work until seven in the evening. They were paid a fixed wage, and some of them chose to work overtime as needed.

A local businessman once had some car trouble on the freeway and brought his car to our garage. It took a total of three hours for the car to be fixed (it was a unique piece of machinery and first of its kind, given it had an advanced processor). During those three hours, I learned some of the most priceless lessons in feature negotiation and bug fixing that are missed greatly in software development.

Jack, our star technician, saw the car being pulled in and immediately worked his way towards it. He wished John, the driver, a good morning, and asked, "What seems to be the problem?"John replied, "Well, I'm here because the car is overheating, and the red light on my dashboard is lit up. I am not sure what that indicates."

I started helping John with the paperwork and asked him to sit in the customer service area, which provided him a full view of the workshop. We had a dozen cars already, which was far above our hourly limit, but John was a long-time customer, providing us a steady line of business with all four of his family's cars. Each hour, more cars came in; some were walk-ins, and others had scheduled maintenance appointments.

The garage could accommodate eight cars at any one time, and had five technicians that were professionals in different parts of the vehicle. One of the technicians was Jack, who was also training two recent hires, and they would occasionally seek his advice as they worked on a few models.

It was nine thirty in the morning, and John wanted to get to Cheeko by noon, which was 45 miles away. How long will it take to repair his car? Jack started the diagnosis and came back with a list of things that were wrong.

1. The light was on due to needing an oil change, which would take around 30 minutes and cost $80 for the premium oil.

2. Overheating was due to thermostat wear and tear and would need to be replaced. This would take at least two hours and be dependent on finding the right thermostat in the auto shop across the street. If it was not available, we would need to order it from another auto store five miles away, and it would take at least 45 minutes for it to be delivered. The associated costs would total $300.

3. In addition to this, Jack also noticed that the air conditioning was due for service. This would take 30 minutes to refill the cooling gas, but this was not an urgent problem. The costs would total $150.

4. One of the wiper blades was worn and no longer functioning properly. It would take 15 minutes to fix and cost about $20.

By the time this assessment was documented, five more cars had pulled into the garage with all sorts of issues. The total number of cars was 17 by 10 AM, and we hadn't even fixed one car.

John, the driver of our first car, made the choice to just do the thermostat replacement, oil change, and wiper replacement. He then asked, "Can we start them in parallel?" Jack said, "No. Since we are changing the thermostat, we have a dependency for this to be completed before changing the oil. So you'll need to wait between 2 hours and 45 minutes to 3 hours and 15 minutes." John asked Jack to get started while he made a few calls to his business in Cheeko to let them know he would be running late 10 additional cars pulled into the driveway. There was no more available space in the waiting lot of the garage. Three of the cars were VIP customers and they all wanted Jack's attention now. There was a total of 27 cars by 10:15 AM, and we had not even delivered the first car. Everyone wanted triage with an exact amount of time it would take to fix their cars. This was also day one on the job for me, and the atmosphere in the workshop by 10:30 AM was complete chaos.

Mike, a senior manager at the workshop, called his elder brother, Stan, who was on call to provide additional support for such days. Luckily, Stan was available and would be at the workshop in 30 minutes. By the time Stan arrived, we had 32 cars in the queue and only two completed.

Jack hadn't further looked at John's car since he was waiting on the thermostat from across town, and was helping triage other cars. John had been waiting quietly, but now his patience was beginning to wear thin.

Of the two brothers, Stan was more experienced, having worked with Toyota and General Motors. He was well versed with improving focus and getting more done. Stan had put up a sign for all the technicians that read, "Stop starting and start finishing." His mantra was, "Don't start work on a car unless you know you can finish it." This morning, we had ignored this process philosophy as it didn't seem practical for real life scenarios.

Fast forwarding on to the present years, I work as a Project Manager at a candy company, where the IT department is constantly in a similar scenario, with limited workforce, small environment, and a fixed timeline. There are multiple stakeholders in the business, some of which are VIPs who have to be in the market by a certain date due to business goals, objectives, and even competition. The problems are exactly the same: ongoing bugs that cause much re-work, aggravation, high failure rates on projects, and unhappy customers.

I keep thinking of applying the fundamentals utilized in the auto workshop years ago, which are still fresh in my memory. This month, my IT department, which has 300 engineering and 10 management staff, was behind schedule on 90 percent of our commitments to our business. Our engineering head was warned to deliver this year's goals, or face a 70 percent budget reduction toward innovation plans for the company.

The scenario was far more complicated, of course, as the politics on a garage floor are almost non-existent compared to a corporate powerhouse. A general risk that organizations face is a downward spiral, eventually going out of business if they do not learn quickly from their failures. Failure is imminent, but it's important to learn from mistakes in order to succeed sooner. If this does not happen, organizations quickly dwindle. This is unfortunately the fate that many companies experience and can be totally prevented. There are very simple means to avoiding wasting trillions of dollars in failed IT projects.

A general risk that organizations face is a downward spiral, eventually going out of business if they do not learn quickly from their failures.

Lesson Learned:

Don't disregard the skills and practices you learned at your old job. Instead, find a new way to utilize them. The company might be different, but the problems are often the same.

The Apprentice and the Project Manager

2 Process Monkey

Tweet: *Demand is a double-edged sword. If you aren't mindful of it, you will lose your competitive advantage. @ApprenticePM*

On a day like today, all the technicians in the workshop were discouraged at seeing the work pile up. They had faith in their abilities, but were not able to see through the clutter of highly demanding customers toward what could be done to improve the situation. Two car owners threatened to walk away permanently if Jack did not start work on their cars right away.

Stan walked in and with a highly engaging smile, said, "Good morning! We will attend to all of you as soon as possible, and get you where you need to be in time or provide alternate accommodation for your needs as an intermediate measure. Please be patient with us for 20 to 30 minutes."

Stan worked his way to Jack, who was still not finished working on John's car, and said, "Good morning, Jack. It looks like we have reached a boiling point today, how can I help you?" Jack said, "Good morning, Stan. I am working through this engine and I will be done in five minutes when the new guy will take over. We are doing everything possible here, and I have told your brother we need to expand and get more hands. This demand is way ahead of our capacity. It's good you are here, maybe you can talk some sense into him."

Mike's wife called him, giving word that he had to leave for rest of the day due to an emergency at home. I helped Stan get set up for rest of his day.

Stan was intently studying a whiteboard, and then asked if he could clean it up and use the space. I said he could, and helped him out.

In a few minutes, the whiteboard had a small table at the top right hand side that read:

Technicians	5
Cars in capacity per hour	8
Time per car	Average 1 hour
Max waiting time once work had begun in the last hour	1 hour for John's car
Waiting on parts	Thermostat
Time to triage	5 minutes (Jack + TBD)
Missed commitment	John's car

Stan assigned me the task of keeping this small performance board updated every hour throughout the day. He also asked me to ensure that with each hour, we *reduced the average time per car and minimized waiting time once work had begun.*

My iPhone came in handy to keep a track of each technician and measure their cycle time. Stan located the yellow book, which was buried in his brother's office, and went to find the materials manager, Steve.

The yellow book was a knowledge resource from the past that had been filled with checklists on the parts needed for each sort of repair. The technicians did not want to carry the book around, and would simply guess which caused them to miss out on the parts or get the wrong ones, thus increasing the wait times. The book was so heavy that it ended up being shelved, and no one ever used it.

Steve was updating the inventory of parts received, and Stan inquired about the thermostat that had still not arrived. Steve had already called the store twice; they said it was on its way.

The auto shop had a few spare cars for emergency purposes. Stan decided to give one to John so he would not be further delayed. John said that he would be back by four PM and to please ensure his car would be ready by then or he would have to find some other shop to fix this problem. Stan assured John that would not be necessary, and sent him on his way.

Steve needed to ensure that our technicians used the yellow book more often so we didn't order the wrong parts or forget any during the first order.

This was done by figuring out the most common checklists needed, and putting them on a big printout in the shop, which was more useful than carrying the entire book.

Once work began, the maximum waiting time in the last hour soon went down to nearly zero, and the cars started to get done substantially faster. The morale of the technicians went up, and we had just got through the first set of issues for the day.

Technicians	5
Cars in capacity per hour	8
Time per car	Average 1 hour
Max waiting time once work had begun in the last hour	2 hours for John's car but 0 for others
Waiting on parts	Thermostat still not available
Time to triage	3 minutes (Jack + new guy)
Missed commitment	John's car

Steve started to do something really unique. He not only treated the cars as an important priority, but also each technician. They became very important stakeholders for Steve of equal weight as the customers. He ensured that the technicians were pre-supplied with the necessary parts for each car prior to starting work. The coordination between Steve and the technicians was similar to a symphony orchestra.

By this time, we had 18 cars complete and out of the door, yet still had a queue, which had grown to 50 cars. It was three PM, and it seemed like we would never catch up before the day ended.

The thermostat finally arrived and all hands were on deck for John's car, which was finished by four PM, only minutes before John arrived. This caused the wait time to jump up for the other cars, though the morale was still great after having finally completed the work on John's car.

By four PM, the data showed as:

Technicians	5
Cars in capacity per hour	8
Time per car	Average 1.5 hours
Max waiting time once work had begun in the last hour	4 hour for John's car but 40 minutes for others
Waiting on parts	
Time to triage	3 minutes (Jack + New Guy)
Missed commitment	John's car

It was clear we would have 20 cars queued up from today for tomorrow.

At the end of the day, Stan called in all the technicians and Steve for an overall briefing and what could be done better for tomorrow, since we now had a tremendous backlog along with expected new demand for tomorrow.

The debrief resulted in significant gratitude for the team of technicians, who had achieved 40% more productivity than other normal days, and Steve was sincerely appreciated by everyone in the partnership. We then worked on an action plan for the next morning so as to get ahead of the demand. It was strange to realize how demand was a double-edged sword. If we weren't mindful of demand, we would be submerged in no time, and no longer have any competitive advantage and thus start losing business.

It was strange to realize how demand was a double-edged sword. If we weren't mindful of demand, we would be submerged in no time, and no longer have any competitive advantage and thus start losing business.

Coming back to the present, being a Project Manager at a candy company, our priority was the Halloween candy spike, which was only 45 days away, and the peak code freeze began in the next seven days. Along with this, we had a set of new software updates and marketing campaigns, in order to bring in new vendors and customers to our website. I made a list of all that was expected from the engineering teams. They were self-sufficient in managing their tasks, but needed an overall focus on their priorities for the present.

I came up with 55 changes expected in the next seven days before hitting our peak freeze at 12 engineering teams. Even if they worked full time at 80 hours per person per week, we would not get 10% of these initiatives completed.

What was killing us was the wait time at various stages of the value stream – waiting for hardware, waiting for business requirements, and waiting for environments. Typically, each engineer was allocated to four or more projects that they were working on, along with supporting issues that came up in production.

I went looking for Lynda and found her in a meeting with her boss on similar topics. I said, "Lynda, I am pretty sure you are aware we are not going to be meeting our commitments to the business in the next seven days."

Lynda was a lean portfolio expert. We sat and re-arranged the data to be as below:

Engineering teams	12 teams and 4 project managers
Cycle time per team to deliver a feature	3 days to 14 days
# of features	55

Max waiting time once work had begun in the last day (for environments or data refreshes)	6 hours
Waiting on storage	2 weeks
Time to support production issues per team	10 hours per week
Missed commitment	Marketing campaign for early bird attraction

On a philosophical level, one of the reasons why people hate processes is because process efficiency is hidden or never measured. If teams are focused on the metrics derived above, the confidence in processes will be greater.

Lynda and I decided to pull key leads of the teams to a debrief and develop an action plan of what could be achieved in the next seven days.

Here was the action plan:

- Identify the cause for wait time on environments and the process lags to get one. Define a heightened alertness process that kicks in 20 minutes after environment issue has been flagged.

- Identify storage needs for next four months and pre-order the same.

- Reduce cycle time per team to be three to seven days in lieu of three days to 14 days by reducing the number of features in progress. Swarming on the high value features first. Any feature slipping its cycle time commitments must be prioritized to ensure commitments are met as agreed.

- Define minimum capacity needs for Halloween and launch immediately. Plan a backup upgrade two weeks before Halloween.

Why do most debriefs fail?

The team goes through many courage-finding exercises to identify the blockers, and if they see no progress, the debrief meetings fail.

The goal of every organization should be to establish a fast feedback loop to quickly fail and learn, or to succeed even quicker. Debriefs with teams help swarm the problems and develop effective action plans in real life, it is the lack of rigor in executing actions that causes any process improvements to fail.

Lesson Learned:

The problem of demand exceeding supply can be solved with a little mathematics and a lot of motivation. Make sure to always prioritize the needs of your team, and brief them completely. Allow them to be a part of your action plan, and coordinate accordingly.

The Apprentice and the Project Manager

3 The Journey to a Positive "NO"

Tweet: *It is better to say NO to one client than to risk losing your entire business by taking on too much work. @ApprenticePM*

One of the earliest lessons I learned from working with Stan that I remember was, "If you have to say NO and know that the consequences are going to be bad, then find someone else to say NO for you." That someone is usually the customer themselves.

So we had carryover from yesterday and more to be queued today. How were we going to fix this problem? Stan had a simple solution: Let's reserve 40% of our capacity for pre-booked work that is by appointment, and 40% as a drive in without appointment. The remaining 20% would be reserved to improve our daily flow to make us even more productive.

Jack asked Stan, "Now why would the customers take an appointment before coming to us rather than just go to another car workshop?" Stan smiled and replied, "We will assure the customer in and out times for standard services.

In addition to this, we will give them a stop discount of 10% on any spare parts we may use. This can be written off. If the customers still choose to come here without an appointment, then we can provide them express service for 20% increase in cost for things that can be done through appointments. This will only work if we provide excellent service for our customers whose appointments are within two days of their calling. We can also hire a driver to pick up and drop off the cars booked by appointment, a service which our customers would love. It is very difficult to say NO to a customer once he has already arrived at the workshop then if he is on the phone, where you can give him a more meaningful answer along with NO."

It is very difficult to say NO to a customer once he has already arrived at the workshop then if he is on the phone, where you can give him a more meaningful answer along with NO.

Steve jumped in and said, "This will not only help us book appointments, but also predict demand up front, so we can order spare parts or have them on standby before time." It was a win-win for everyone.

The team sat down and made five lots in the morning as reserved for booking, starting with the next week. As demand for reserved time grew, they would eventually increase the reserved time boxes to 14 per day, based on all other capacity.

When the customer service started to market this new process, it worked from the beginning as the customers saved a lot of unnecessary wait time and loved the addition of 10% discount on parts.

In the present years, I thought of how I could use Stan's fundamental approach to my IT organization. Obviously, I could not ask my stakeholders to take appointments, nor did I have the authority to offer a 10% discount on software development. The problems were very similar, but the approach used in the auto workshop did not apply in the IT organization. I again sat down with Lynda to tell her the story of that experience, and she decided to give it a shot. We booked time for lunch the next day to go through different models that could give them the same outcome.

On my way back home, while waiting for my train to arrive, I realized a straight forward solution to my problem. I would need classes of service. Using trains as my example, I would need classes of trains with some that stopped at every stop, some with only two stops, and some that had four stops.

The next day, I explained to Lynda my observation, and we sat down to define the various classes of service that we would need to better the service of our own organization. We ended up with four classes:

Class Type	Description
Rapid delivery expected in 1 week or less on work packages that are small sized	Queue up this work for a rapid task force team that can quickly turn around on small sized high value work
Work package needing 2-4 weeks without infrastructure enhancements	Queue this work for enhancement teams who often rotate resource with rapid task force
Innovative work needed for growth	Queue work for consistent development teams defined at the beginning of the year

Infrastructure enhancements for holiday capacity	Define an active team round the year solely treating each day as a holiday and ensuring that we as an organization are ready every day, not just on holidays

There was one problem with the approach. What if the queue became extensive and the wait times exponential? Whether a train stopped at all stops or at limited ones, it was still the same size. So the size of the teams would need to be standardized in order to be predictable on the capacity. Secondly, we would need to identify the work in progress limit for each team, without which the entire purpose of improving focus would be lost.

Lynda and I identified the number of people needed per team, and observed in a limited wait time environment. The queue size was limited to two features, but any time the wait time increased, the queue size would increase, which would cause heightened alertness and we would act on limiting the wait time.

The portfolio management process, designed on service classes or queues, team capacity, or simply the number of teams and innovation, increased our productivity almost immediately. There was one problem though. After a few weeks of steady performance, our queue sizes and lead times started to increase again. Puzzled, Lynda and I started to recapture all statistics, and this is what it looked like:

Class Type	Description	Service Level when started	Service Level today
Rapid delivery expected in 1 week or less on work packages that are small sized	Queue up this work for a rapid task force team that can quickly turn around on small sized high value work	97%	80%
Work package needing 2-4 weeks without infrastructure enhancements	Queue this work for enhancement teams who often rotate resource with rapid task force	90%	70%

Innovative work needed for growth	Queue work for consistent development teams defined at the beginning of the year	Still to be calculated	Still to be calculated
Infrastructure enhancements for holiday capacity	Define an active team round the year solely treating each day as a holiday and ensuring that we as an organization are ready every day, not just on holidays	70%	30%

If we had met our commitments 97% of the time a few weeks ago, we were now down to 80% for the rapid delivery work.

We decided to jump in and do another debrief with the teams.

Here was the set of findings and actions:

1. Now that everyone understood the service queues, the teams were being forced to accept work beyond their capacity. The teams were being penalized by their stakeholders to accept more work, which was reducing the overall "output."

2. The comparison between two work packages within a service queue was nonexistent. Anyone who shouted the loudest got the priority. This resulted in switching costs and poor quality.

The question in front of us was now clearer – How do we prioritize a queue? How do we establish a threshold level to say NO without burning our relationship with the stakeholders?

Lesson Learned:

Allow your customers to understand your rate of supply versus their demand. Presenting them with options makes it easier for you to say – and for them to accept – the answer of NO. Your business and your team take priority over a single client. Find a way to increase productivity without sacrificing the welfare of your employees or the integrity of your company.

4 Strategically Re-invest/Pivot

Tweet: *Your goal is keep the demand queue prioritized based on a value model that is understood by your team and customers. @ApprenticePM*

We had no luck in solving the question – How do we prioritize the queue? That evening, I flew to New Jersey, and at the gate of the airport, I hailed for a cab. My hotel was two miles away from the airport. The cab driver asked me where I needed to go. I gave him the address and he said, "NO." I was surprised by his response and he went onto say that he had been in queue for 40 minutes and did not want a ride so short unless I was willing to pay him at least $30.

I was three hours ahead of Lynda due to the different time zones, and knew she would still be in the office. I left her a voice message on a possible solution: We will say NO based on the dollar value associated with each project.

Over the weekend, I went over everything we had learned in the last few weeks and came up with a more comprehensive solution. The four value model questions that I developed were:

1. Can we kill this project? If not, what do we get for it?

2. Compared to others in the queue, how does it compare?

3. Is a Net Present Value calculation possible? Or any sensible value outcome? Do we get funds left in innovation budget?

4. What if we delay this project to the next in line work package?

On Monday, Lynda and I met over coffee and reviewed the end-to-end situation. We added two more questions to the above:

5. Does this project align with business strategy?

6. What is the minimum viable product we may sponsor for now?

The teams reviewed these questions and added that we must replace the item in progress if another priority comes up.

We decided to test drive the new value framework at our next project intake meeting. The product managers were puzzled at the filters and wanted to know if it came from the senior management. Lynda looked at them and said something remarkable: "This is what we need to be successful, and please feel free to check in with your management on your value models before you bring them here for project intake." Then she went on to give an example of how a TV remote had more than 70 features that were never utilized. "Seeing value is our first responsibility and anything that is not value is waste. Unfortunately, waste causes more waste than we can imagine."

One Senior Product Manager who had been with the company was visibly upset on hearing this, and said, "My business needs this by end of the month, and you are asking me to waste time over your unnecessary questions and not be worried about my end stakeholders?"

Lynda sympathized with the Senior Product Manager and let her finish her statement before smiling and saying, "I know this sounds like a lot of effort, but in reality, it is simple and can be done in less than a few minutes. Let me help you." In less than five minutes, the senior product manager had the reasons and data on why she was making a poor choice for her stakeholders. She thanked Lynda and went on with her list for the day.

Although it seemed like only a small win that day, the organization moved in a new direction from then on. Lynda grew ever more confident and enjoyed supporting her colleagues on the value model. The development teams quickly learned that the value models could be adapted to their needs as long as they had clarity of the vision and strategy of the organization.

Back in the days of being an apprentice, I recollect that Stan declined car makes other than Toyota, Honda, and Ford, as we had limited skill and the investment needed to capture the market was beyond our business strategy.

We often said NO to cars if the investment to repair would outweigh the value the customer would eventually get from the decision. We sometimes offered help in referring reliable newer model cars or even used cars.

If the priority needed to be swapped, we kept the customers informed on the impact and generally followed it with an extra credit on customer service. At times, we threw in a free wash and wax for an extra two hour wait time.

Our value at the auto shop was, "Customer delight at lightning speed with accurate service."

Our VIP customers would get "super express" service, but pay a premium price for it. Usually, this included an offered pick-up and drop-off at home, periodic reminders of service, and the ability to exchange vehicles for long term faults at minimal prices.

The eventual goal was to reduce work in progress and keep the queue prioritized based on a value model that was understood not only by the team, but also by all stakeholders (including the customers).

The eventual goal was to reduce work in progress and keep the queue prioritized based on a value model that was understood not only by the team, but also by all stakeholders (including the customers).

In addition to the value model used for prioritization, the auto shop kept a record of service needs and completions of the cars. If a problem was recurring, then a permanent solution would be sought or free service was completed each time, as a means to compensate on the time the auto was off the road.

Each technician had a clear idea on value being added for every car they serviced and the history of the vehicle.

Lesson Learned:

Say NO if the investment will outweigh the value that the customer or company will receive. Value models can be adapted to your needs provided you have clarity of vision and understanding of your organization's strategy. Anything without value is waste, which will only cause more waste.

5 Piling Debt Needs to Be Paid Off

Tweet: **A simple quality check built within teams ensures high quality product. @ApprenticePM**

Being a Project Manager had its own level of visibility. Today, we were called for a priority meeting with the engineering head of the company. "Ladies and gentlemen – we have a crisis situation. Seven minutes ago, our site was hacked and user IDs and passwords were stolen. Our monitoring systems were able to pick that up and lock down the site immediately. The hacker sent the data to the local newspaper, and we have made the news headline. While we work through this crisis, I need you to direct any media queries to me alone."

Then, as if this was not enough, he pointed at me and asked me to come to his office. I was sure everyone in the room thought it was something my team had done. Not being able to hide the emotion on my face, I went to the office of the engineering head, and we discussed the remediation plan.

He said that the information security teams were able to check our vulnerability report and have figured out the issue. A developer was on it and would be deploying the fix to test in a few minutes. He also wanted to know what my thoughts were on how to avoid such incidents in the future and what we learned from this episode collectively.

The support manager then knocked on the door to tell us that the problem had been fixed. He also informed us of additional monitoring that had been added to ensure we pick up this issue in seconds and that there is now automated tracking of any hackers without the site shutting down or losing vulnerable information. The engineering head sighed with relief.

The next day, we deployed monitoring information radiators by every team's sitting area, so they were aware of the quality of product being produced. It was a huge win for developers to start improving quality and security without the QA or the Information Security asking them to do so at the last minute.

Some developers started a mock contest that whoever gets the most bug points and vulnerability alerts buys lunch for the team. This one issue made us learn as a company how a simple quality check built within teams ensures high quality product. They made it a point to add monitoring to everything that was being developed, not just for security reasons, but also to track the value in the production environment. We started to be a very empirical decision maker, which was welcome by the organization.

Back at the workshop, a similar incident happened when Stan received a call from one of our customers that morning. He came into the workshop area and called for a quick meeting. All of us were surprised by the debrief as it was not even mid-day yet. Stan broke the news of how one of our customers had just survived an accident, the reason for which was brake failure. The brakes had been serviced today by one of our new guys. Initial reports filed indicated technical error in brake alignment, which caused excess pressure and eventual brake failure. They also discovered that the brake oil was very low and should have been caught by the technician. Overall, we could have avoided this near fatal experience for one of our valued customers. On identifying the problem, it was clear that the handoff from one technician to another was not always accurate, and relied on personal capacity and will. Stan left the problem with the team and asked them to come up with a suitable solution on how this incident could be avoided in the future.

The technicians returned to work without an immediate solution, and Stan stood there watching their work habits and styles. Somewhere was a very distressed customer, and he was responsible for their problems. Steve, our resource manager, came and asked Stan if he could offer a small change. He suggested that after every service, there would be another person who would review the work and sign it off before delivering it to the customer. Stan argued that this would slow us down and potentially would not be visible to the customer.

Steve replied that it might slow us down in the beginning, but soon enough it would be like a ritual, and the technicians would adapt it into their daily flow. We would pair them for reviewing each other's work, which would potentially also avoid re-work if found by the customer. Overall, the eventual benefits would outweigh the overhead. Why not try it for a week before developing it as the norm?

The next day, each technician had a training partner, and they started to practice this change. In the beginning, almost every one complained, but by lunch break, they were used to it. At the end of the day, there was a buzz in the garage, similar to bee hives, where the conversation was about how they were spotting each other's strengths and weaknesses, how they were learning better practices from each other, and how each one of them was becoming strong.

Stan had taken a more full-time role managing the workshop, while his brother supported the other job across town. We were enjoying learning from him and Steve every day.

There is no replacement for "pairing" in any product development or service delivery. Overall, it beats two single person(s) outcomes by leaps and bounds.

By the end of the month, we had serviced 50% more autos, and also improved on the quality metrics and lowered the amount of re-work to negligible.

One unique quality we realized quickly was that it was critical to work with a lot of empathy in the service industry, and hiring folks who were short on empathy would result in eventual degradation of customer service. We might have figured out many technical means, but it was empathy that led us to the epiphany of providing for the customer's most important needs, even if it was to understand possible defects in the system before handing it over to the users for further testing. Stan started to personally test drive the cars before asking the owner to drive it to confirm if everything "felt" good to them.

One unique quality we realized quickly was that it was critical to work with a lot of empathy in the service industry, and hiring folks who were short on empathy would result in eventual degradation of customer service.

Stan started to document specific tests for every scenario, so that other technicians could test drive the cars with a check list. The idea was to assume that the test would fail. That way, the technician who was responsible for fixing the car knew exactly the tests that it needed to pass, and thus, was more accurate in repairs.

At first, I thought the cost of the development would skyrocket, but it did not. In fact, it reduced the time to give the car back to the customers, as well as the cycle time, due to standardized reviewing practices which earlier did not happen or were in effective, causing a lot of rework.

With a little bit of automation of test cases, the benefits can be enormous on overall quality and cycle time for services or products.

By making quality of in-progress products visible, companies can save tremendous costs in major bugs that creep into the end systems. Quality metrics must be visible to everyone in the company. Every department should maintain and publish a cycle time for services they offer, including quality control. Metrics help inspire a change in behavior which further helps form habits when repeated as needed.

Lesson Learned:

You might have figured out the technical aspects of a problem, but it is empathy that will allow you to provide for the customer's most important needs, even if only to understand possible defects in the system. Ensuring quality within your company will ensure quality in your products.

6 Mr. Grumpy's Driver

Tweet: *People who abuse their administrative power harm the entire company. Your team will show you real value. @ApprenticePM.*

We were proud to be servicing one of the wealthiest families in the city. The only problem was that the usual owners were grumpy when their wheels are in the shop, and their drivers were doing the rounds to have them fixed.

The replacement cars were usually not the ones they were used to. Stan introduced a means to improve customer satisfaction by providing on-premise service for smaller issues for a premium rate that not only provided the visibility to the owner of the car being worked on and being fixed, but also improved confidence in excellent customer service. The usual price for such service was five times the normal with no wait time. If the car needed to be eventually taken to the shop, it was understandable, as not everything could be done at the owners' estates.

This also avoided dealing with drivers who were not transparent about the real issues in front of the owner. When the cars started to be serviced onsite, these drivers were pitching in to help the technician, rather than simply being another status person. The drivers started to get involved in simple jobs such as clean up, checking the fluids, test driving, holding the tools, and more. This increased the driver's knowledge of the cars, and eventually improved their driving skills, which significantly reduced the amount of wear and tear.

In IT shops, it is often the case that the administrative staff of senior management uses their clout to push things to the front of the queue without paying a premium, causing hampered service to the rest of the company, who may have higher value to be offered. Of course, not all companies face this problem. But we know some companies have folks demanding for exec status every day, if not every hour. We have seen controlling personalities be on top of all situations almost to the point where it becomes unhealthy.

In IT shops, it is often the case that the administrative staff of senior management uses their clout to push things to the front of the queue without paying a premium, causing hampered service to the rest of the company, who may have higher value to be offered.

One such department that often gets pushed to the wall is IT operations - from a simple laptop fix or email problem, to spinning up a virtual machine for a test environment that needs to be escalated.

Operations is usually the panacea where most problems eventually end up and are solved. Operations is also the group that witnesses the heaviest IT turnover in terms of staffing, due to insurmountable pressure. While the problems here are almost all urgent, the best that can be done to alleviate the problem is to make the department invisible and integrate it with the rest of the organization. Slice Operations, and add it to the core delivery organization for not all, but some key functions, which cause bottlenecks. Solve for bottlenecks!

For example, every developer must know how to configure his own build pipeline and avoid dependency on the release engineer in Operations, or provide a read-only access for developers to debug issues so that they reduce dependency on Operations engineers for simple debugging tasks.

To make the Operations department invisible means to find 20% of skills that can be imparted to developers, and establish a means to regulate this through configuration management tools to avoid other surprises.

Besides this, the service desk and the rest of operations team must re-think their contracts. The contracts, if need be, have to conform to some sort of service level negotiation framework, and not service level agreements.

Lesson Learned:

Convert constraints into strategic levers in order to identify and minimize waste. Involving Operations in development processes may reduce quality issues, rework costs, and allow for focus on the right priorities.

7 Attack Tree

Tweet: **The best way to deal with a threat toward your company is to get ahead of it. @ApprenticePM**

Every time we had a newer version car, it was always a problem to know if we were breaking something that made the vehicle more vulnerable to burglar attacks. For example, if we fixed a door issue, we may not have correctly reset the security alert system, which would cause the alarm to not go off if someone was trying to tamper with the door handle.

Since the parts were available in a variety of different qualities, with instructions that ranged from simple steps to complex, five page directions, it was always difficult to guess if what we had done was accurate.

One of the drivers brought back his car that had been serviced for a sliding window problem the day before, saying the security system was not working. The technicians fixed the problem in a matter of seconds and added it to their "attack tree" log, which was going to become one of the standards later in our auto workshop.

Years later, when I had the Quality department of the candy company constantly complain about how the developers were introducing vulnerabilities into our code and that they needed to be fixed yesterday, it made me think of the scenario at the auto workshop.

One of the QA leaders came up to me after a horrible meeting summarizing the vulnerabilities our developers were introducing that made our products prone to attacks such as SQL injection. He added that it is clear our developers are probably not even sure that they are causing this problem and it sounds like an education issue.

I had learned from a close family friend who worked for the Special Forces that the best way to deal with a threat is to get ahead of it.

So how do we deal with a situation that a developer is unintentionally writing code that is making our products vulnerable? We started a system of recording every attack on our website, calling it an "attack tree", then challenged developers to come up with one to two line code fixes for these problems. We slowly automated the process of analysis and recommendations with emergent tools from the market. Eventually, we were able to help developers understand the problem even before creating it. Every time we encountered something new, we added to our attack tree, which became our master robot, or "terminator," to make our system more secure.

For every line of code we wrote, we had the means to test it against the 3000 plus test cases based on the attack tree. If there was critical vulnerability cited, we had a knowledge repository on how to identify code that was causing the problem and how to fix it.

If there was critical vulnerability cited, we had a knowledge repository on how to identify code that was causing the problem and how to fix it.

Lesson Learned:

Be conscious of your company's weaknesses and plan for mistakes. The best defence is offense, so create a plan of attack to prevent vulnerabilities before they happen. Document past mistakes and learn from them.

8 Lean Infrastructure

Tweet: *Identify a team to work on a problem, and let them define the path toward improvement. @ApprenticePM*

After being promoted to a VP of Infrastructure, one of my primary challenges was getting greater scalability, peak season after peak season. The scale of the problems was 20 times larger than when I was a Project Manager. In addition to this, some strange consultants kept lecturing us to "be Agile," "be Lean," etc.

What they were telling us, in short, was to apply the auto shop processes to the grander scale of 100 people infrastructure organization of the candy company.

The issue here was that the most of my middle management was dealing with a blocked mindset since they had been there and done that. They didn't believe in streamline processes or being more accountable for their actions.

The question I had in my full list of never ending problems was: Where do I start? In addition to this, the immense amount of variability across my teams for building basic hardware was going to be a major issue to gain agility.

The answer turned out to be simple - start in an area of maximum opportunity, identify a team to work on the problem, and let them define the path toward improvement. I personally did not have the capacity to be the process guy to fix these things. In addition to this, there was the VP of Process and Tools who was talking about automation of all Infrastructure services, but the basic issue here was that we had too much variability and automating too many different ways of doing things that would hamper agility.

My predecessor had tried Agile and Lean and Kanban principles, but nothing had really worked. Instead, the teams were more frustrated, due to change fatigue.

What I set out to do was radically different from my predecessor...

I defined clear objectives to bring consistency to our world in order to reduce variability around building server hardware:

1. Create a value stream for the end-to-end process, from ordering to usage of the servers.

2. Identify nuances around different processes that could be due to different manufacturing sources; e.g. AIX, HP, and Sun/Oracle, etc.

   a. Do the financials

   b. Order a box

   c. Receive it

   d. Rack it

   e. Cable it

   f. Base image (AIX/ patches), etc.

   g. Network configuration

   h. Identify any collaboration needs with security or facilities

3. Optimize this value stream.

4. Automate around optimized processes.

5. Move away from wasteful conversations and focus on what sort of services are needed for the applications – for example, high availability.

This would make many people uncomfortable, so the vision was changed to be, "simplify and automate."

Laying out the steps as above would clearly help bring visibility and measurements. Soon, teams were making their value stream maps and keeping these up to date through collaboration, which caused innovative simplification.

Example Value Stream Map

Infrastructure organizations are plagued by a huge turnaround times that throw major initiatives off track. This stalls the growth of an organization. Imagine a development team needing a Red Hat VM created for development work. This would traditionally take up to 25 days and even more if there are defects.

Drawing a simple value stream, the time to value is 25 days, which is not good for today's rapidly changing enterprise.

The same service request can now be cut short to a more manageable time frame, due to the advent of automation and configuration management tooling taking our data centre management to the next level.

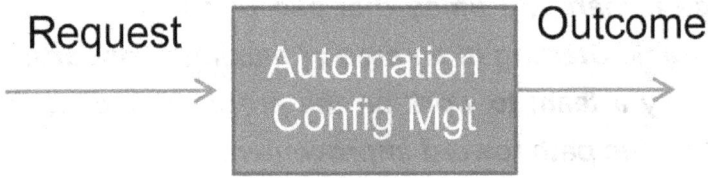

Request   **Automation Config Mgt**   Outcome

The long pole of waiting for a sysadmin, network engineer, or storage engineer to monitor their parts is now fully automated through Configuration Management. This cuts the manual deployment and waiting times from 25 days to about 30 minutes. The approval cycle is the same. The time to value for servicing infrastructure service requests has dropped by at least 80% of initial required time, along with tremendous savings in human resource costs.

We are moving towards a cloud mentality and need to empower the developers; basically, get out of their way!

We are moving towards a cloud mentality and need to empower the developers; basically, get out of their way!

Increase in positional authority also increases complexity and variability of problems to be solved. Leaders identify patterns and use these to achieve mindset change.

Lesson Learned:

Infrastructure organizations are often plagued by huge turnaround times that can throw your initiative off track. Starting in an area of maximum opportunity, identify a team to work on the problem, and let them define the path toward improvement.

9 Financial Health Check

Tweet: *Identifying your assets and liabilities will allow you to determine your equity - your overall worth as a company. @ApprenticePM*

Understanding the balance sheet is important because it needs to be managed on an ongoing basis, and not act as a lag indicator at the end of the month/quarter/ annual. This is also termed as foundations of financial engineering.

It starts with a given budget, or a dollar amount that is available for spending, though that does not mean it will be spent.

We figure out our current sources of revenue. These are often called "assets", examples of which include available cash, your current sales channels, website, etc. The initial dollar amount provided by your corporate finance every year is your asset in terms of available cash.

We also determine our current liabilities, which are economic obligations that need to be paid off to someone else. For example, building a new office will need a loan amount. This known loan amount will become a liability. Salaries to be paid to employees are another form of liability.

Finally, we figure our equity. Equity is our value as judged by others. Our goal should be to have a higher equity. Equity is also described as what we are worth.

$$Assets - Liability = Equity$$

Every project executed should be judged in terms of improving equity, even if it is in terms of innovation. Value models are the means to understanding prioritization of initiatives to have a positive impact on the overall equity of the company.

It is important to note that in some businesses, IT costs may eventually be an overall liability, while in others they are always an asset.

As a portfolio think tank team, the goal every year should be to increase the equity of the company. Any time the equity goes negative or drops, that is an indicator that something has gone wrong.

In the candy company, a major decision to expand was withdrawn, as it would hamper the current equity of the company. The expansion plan was to acquire another confectionary company that had recently renewed its technology landscape but was not doing well in terms of business. This confectionary company had changed the technology landscape of its entire online sales channel, but was struggling to get a better business market. Our management team judged the company not only in terms of technology, but also how it would improve the equity of the company and made a final price offer to the confectionary company. Since the deal was no longer lucrative enough, the confectionary company backed out of the deal. A forceful acquisition would have resulted in a drop in the candy company's earnings in the market.

While balance sheets are a lag measure for the market, we started to use them as a real time health check to provide direction to our decisions on investing in newer projects. Every portfolio manager partnered on coming up with the Net Present Value (NPV) for every new project that was being proposed. Soon our balance sheet was demonstrating visible improvements. Financial projections were done on a quarterly basis and updates to those were discussed weekly. Our market commitments were met judiciously. The above financial engineering translates into various minute details within corporate as head count reports, budgets, and monthly projections. The essence of all this is to maintain a positive equity and work on a continuously improving equity. Halloween was a day we looked forward to, as that time of the year, our sales went sky high, thus improving our company's equity.

In the auto work shop, I was fortunate to get an introduction to the daily general ledger that basically followed the same equation as above

$$Assets - Liability = Equity$$

Any new piece of equipment to support further business in terms of reduced time to fix cars was treated as an expense that could be capitalized. As much as possible, our accountant managed to keep expenses on the capitalized side. This helped us depreciate the expenses and improve our net income. This was also called the Income statement. There are mainly Income statements, cash flow statements, and balance sheets that are important for financial engineering.

Simplified Income Statement for Auto Workshop (monthly example):

Sales from fixing 2000 cars= $200,000

Cost of fixing 2000 cars = $80,000 (variable costs)

Cost of standard operation per month = $50,000 (fixed costs)

Gross profit = $70,000

The more cars we were able to fix, the more our profits improved. Buying equipment to help fix cars faster also improved the profit, since we were able to fix more cars. Sometimes we would have marketing expenses, or other miscellaneous expenses.

If we borrowed money from the bank, we would have interest charge, too.

Finally, Net Income was monitored daily through real time financial tracking. In a small business, it is crucial to spend time understanding these numbers, as the net income translates into what cash is available for further operations.

For large corporate balance sheets, income statements and cash flow statements are more complex with fairly more heads of data. However, the basic information looks the same.

Pay attention to the daily financial statistics of your company. The share value and balance sheets are the outcomes of your day-to-day decisions.

Lesson Learned:

As a management professional, it is important to read the financial statements of your company, such as Income statements, cash flow statements, and balance sheets. Remember that assets combined with liabilities equal your equity, and thus, your success as a business. Every project should be judged in terms of improving your equity, and be sure to stay on top of your paperwork.

Conclusion

Tweet: *Innovation by repetition!*
@ApprenticePM

The story in the previous chapters tells us that repetition and learning continuously is imperative to successful innovation in whatever type of job one is in. The apprentice observed Lean principles successfully in action at the auto workshop, and successfully applied the same principles for a different problem set, based on keen powers of observation and determination when becoming a Project Manager at the candy company. On scaling greater leadership roles, the same principles helped with being more successful.

Let us conclude here by considering the cycle of Innovation. Innovation is needed for growth, and growth is essential for survival in today's competitive world.

Flow of Value from Idea (Vision) to Product as quickly as possible is what "Lean" principles are all about. In some cases, there may be no product, but a service outcome. The basic cycle is applicable to complex scenarios, where the path from idea to outcome is not well defined.

Cycle of Innovation -

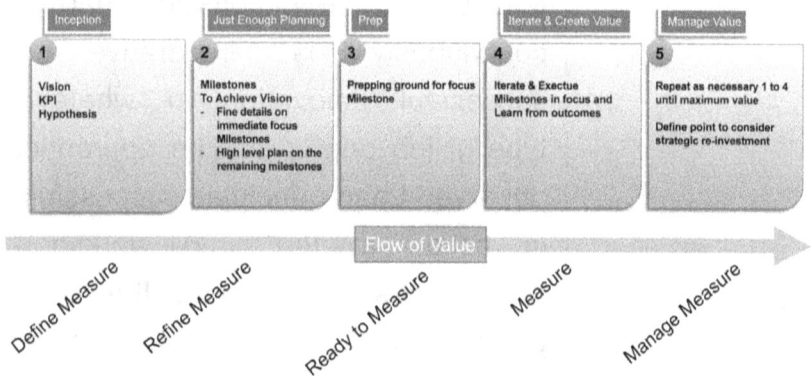

Inception	Just Enough Planning	Prep	Iterate & Create Value	Manage Value
1	**2**	**3**	**4**	**5**
Vision KPI Hypothesis	Milestones To Achieve Vision - Fine details on immediate focus Milestones - High level plan on the remaining milestones	Prepping ground for focus Milestone	Iterate & Exectue Milestones in focus and Learn from outcomes	Repeat as necessary 1 to 4 until maximum value Define point to consider strategic re-investment

Flow of Value →

Define Measure   Refine Measure   Ready to Measure   Measure   Manage Measure

Inception

Vision is the key outcome one plans to get to. In most cases, a Vision may be thought of as a sum of multiple hypotheses together.

Usually a team needs to work on joint visioning together to come up with a hypothesis that needs to be verified.

The optimal means to come up with a vision is a drawing board conversation, and capturing that into a documented format.

Laying out the risks upfront helps ease of tracking the risks to more manageable expectations.

Just Enough Planning

The second most important step in the cycle of Innovation is to define milestones needed to achieve the Vision. There is limited possibility in knowing details around the milestones for the duration of the time it takes to achieve the vision.

However, the team may choose to focus on the next month or two of the work, with fine details around the next 2-4 weeks, versus the future, which is a brief outline. This helps in avoiding excessive and wasteful planning.

Sometimes this is a culture change for companies, as people want to plan budgets in advance for the year. It is important to break free of these paradigms. Budgets are critical, but it is important to look at historic information that basically tells us outcomes achieved after a company has burned through the budget for the year.

Prep

Based on the milestones, there may be prep needed to achieve basic execution discipline and get started.

Iterate & Create Value

Iterations should only be kicked off when the input is known for the iteration. If input to the iteration is not well-thought-out with clearly defined measures, it results in poor performance.

This is very similar to garbage in = garbage out. Usually the quality of input is highly dependent on the previous steps to the cycle of Innovation and repetition.

Managing Value

It is important to identify the outcomes and continuously measure them. There is a point in every product or service when the cost of providing the product or service is comparative to the value delivered. When the product or service begins to deliver only marginal value in terms of outcomes, it is time to consider strategic re-investment of resources and perhaps killing further development. This is also a paradigm shift as we stick to current models of budget, and prefer to spend the entire budget allocated to a specific product or a service.

Through the repetition of steps 1-5, companies and teams are able to fail fast to succeed sooner. It is essential to provide an environment where it is safe to be truthful and allow learning from failure.

The cycle of innovation assures delivering value from concept to product or service as quickly as teams are able to learn from their failures.

Finally, as a ready reference and to re-enforce key takeaway, The Apprentice and the Project Manager teach the following lessons in various chapters of the book.

Key Lessons in the Book:

- Don't disregard the skills and practices you learned at your old job. Instead, find a new way to utilize them. The company might be different, but the problems are often the same.

- The problem of demand exceeding supply can be solved with a little mathematics and a lot of motivation. Make sure to always prioritize the needs of your team, and brief them completely. Allow them to be a part of your action plan, and coordinate accordingly.

- Allow your customers to understand your rate of supply versus their demand. Presenting them with options makes it easier for you to say – and for them to accept – the answer of NO. Your business and your team take priority over a single client. Find a way to increase productivity without sacrificing the welfare of your employees or the integrity of your company.

- Say NO if the investment will outweigh the value that the customer or company will receive. Value models can be adapted to your needs provided you have clarity of vision and understanding of your organization's strategy. Anything without value is waste, which will only cause more waste.

- You might have figured out the technical aspects of a problem, but it is empathy that will allow you to provide for the customer's most important needs, even if only to understand possible defects in the system. Ensuring quality within your company will ensure quality in your products.

- Convert constraints into strategic levers in order to identify and minimize waste. Involving Operations in development processes may reduce quality issues, rework costs, and allow for focus on the right priorities.

- Be conscious of your company's weaknesses and plan for mistakes. The best defense is offense, so create a plan of attack to prevent vulnerabilities before they happen. Document past mistakes and learn from them.

- Infrastructure organizations are often plagued by huge turnaround times that can throw your initiative off track. Starting in an area of maximum opportunity, identify a team to work on the problem, and let them define the path toward improvement.

- As a management professional, it is important to read the financial statements of your company, such as Income statements, cash flow statements, and balance sheets. Remember that assets combined with liabilities equal your equity, and thus, your success as a business. Every project should be judged in terms of improving your equity, and be sure to stay on top of your paperwork.

About the Author

Kamal Manglani is an Agile practitioner and a thought leader in this space. His background is strong, hands-on, practitioner experience delivering cutting-edge technology products in fast-paced Fortune 500 companies. Kamal has successfully implemented Agile across global brands, from US to Europe and Indian Markets. He has pioneered and customized Agile practices within IT infrastructure, applying Lean Kanban principles. Kamal regularly coaches Agile to non-IT-functional areas such as HR and Finance.

www.ingramcontent.com/pod-product-compliance
Lightning Source LLC
Chambersburg PA
CBHW050553280326
41933CB00011B/1822